CONTENTS

Love Little Mix? Want to know EVERYTHING about Perrie, Jade and Leigh-Anne? Then you've totes picked up the right book. Play the puzzles, create new looks for the band and discover something you never knew about our tremendous trio – Little Mix!

P6

6-7	Hey Perrie
8-9	Hey Leigh-Anne!
10-11	Hey Jade!
12-15	Moments in time
16-17	The *Confetti* Tour
18-19	Bye bye, Jesy
20-21	Who's your LM BFF?
22-23	Jade's Star Bakes
25	Mix Kicks
26-27	Little Lyric Mix Up
28-29	*Leigh-Anne: Race, Pop & Power*
30-31	Collaboration Celebration
32-33	WiFi Drop Out
34-35	Walk this way
36-37	Totally random
38-39	Plan the ultimate LM sleepover!
40	Microphone bling
41	Leigh-Anne poster
42-43	DM Dilemmas

P8

44-45   Life in Lockdown

46-47   What's your *Confetti* tour role?

48-49   Perfect pizza topping

50-53   *Little Mix - The Search*

54-55   Create your band

56-57   Twinning

58-59   Who's that Mixer?

60-61   Mixers making it work

62   Album artwork

63   Jade poster

P10

P15

P22

64-65   LM Bullet journal

66-67   The power of three

68-69   Tour threads

70   The search is on

71   All that glitters

72-73   You are everything

74-75   The ultimate Mixer quiz

P48

P66

Published 2021.

Little Brother Books Ltd, Ground Floor,
23 Southernhay East, Exeter, Devon, EX1 1QL

Printed in Poland. ul. Połczyńska 99,01303 Warszawa

LittleBrother
B O O K S

books@littlebrotherbooks.co.uk
www.littlebrotherbooks.co.uk

Hey PERRIE

FULL NAME: Perrie Louise Edwards
DATE OF BIRTH: 10th July, 1993
STAR SIGN: Cancer

GET WEIRD FACT

Perrie has never had a sense of smell!
She had an operation when she was little
to try and correct it, but it didn't work.

CONFETTI CONFESSION

Perrie cried when she saw herself
dressed up as a man for the
Confetti video.

PET PAL

Perrie loves dogs. She has a
Pomeranian named Hatchi and
a French bulldog called Travis.
Hatchi is so famous, he even has
his own Instagram account!
@hatchisgreatadventures.

Family ties

Perrie is really good friends with her brother, Jonnie and she thinks her parents are incredible and supportive. Any chance she gets to spend time with them, she does!

SELF CONFIDENCE

Perrie loves the natural freckles on her face. Her mum calls them 'Angel Kisses!'

Did You Know?

Perrie passed her driving test in January 2020.

Hey LEIGH-ANNE

FULL NAME: Leigh-Anne Pinnock
DATE OF BIRTH: 4th October, 1991
STAR SIGN: Libra

GET WEIRD FACT

Leigh-Anne used to waitress at a pizza restaurant!

CONFETTI CONFESSION

Leigh-Anne reckons the video they made for the single release of *Confetti* is the best they have ever done!

PET PAL

Leigh-Anne is another dog lover. She has an American Pit Bull called Kyro and Harvey, a pug.

Family ties

Leigh-Anne is super-close with her family. Her grandad lives in Jamaica and came to England for the first time to watch Leigh-Anne perform on the *Get Weird* tour - dancing the whole way through! She's also really proud of her mum, who worked her way up to being a supermarket manager, then retrained to be a child protection officer. Leigh-Anne lives her life by the examples her family have set her.

Self Confidence

Leigh-Anne used to worry that her voice wasn't as good as her bandmates, but she's realised she's just as incredible as her fellow Mixers. She has worked hard and hits notes she never thought possible.

Did You Know?

Leigh-Anne used to go to a famous stage school called Sylvia Young. Matt Willis and Rita Ora were also students there!

Hey JADE

FULL NAME: Jade Amelia Thirlwall
DATE OF BIRTH: 26th December, 1992
STAR SIGN: Capricorn

GET WEIRD FACT
Jade says she has never burped in her life!

CONFETTI CONFESSION
Jade loved the creative freedom the band had while creating the *Confetti* album. They pushed boundaries and tried things they never had before.

DID YOU KNOW
Jade is a big fan of Disney and once bought a designer handbag with Bambi on it!

Family ties

Jade idolises her big brother, Karl, who is five years older than her. She also used to think her mum was the legendary Motown singer Diana Ross! It was their support that pushed her to audition for *The X Factor* a third time.

Self Confidence

Jade used to think she wasn't as pretty as the other girls in the band, but now she loves her looks and style.

BOO!

11

Moments
IN TIME

With awards to be won, songs to release and festivals to perform at, the girls are always on the go. Let's take a look at some of the recent highlights from Planet Little Mix.

2011

Four girls entered a singing competition called *The X Factor*. The judges recognised their talents and put them together as a girl band called 'Rythmix'. As the competition went on, it was clear these ladies had something special. They changed their name to Little Mix, crushed it in the final at Wembley Arena and won the show!

2012

The girls released their first album, *DNA*, which reached number two in the charts – not a bad start!

2013

Little Mix became the first British girl group to enter the US top five with their debut single! They also embarked on their first ever tour, The *DNA* Tour, and released their second album, *Salute*.

2014

The band took *Salute* out on tour to play to all their UK fans.

2015

Their third album, *Get Weird*, was released and reached number two in the UK charts, and number one in Ireland!

2016

Glory Days became Little Mix's first number one album! The band also took the album on a 60-date tour.

2017

Little Mix flew off around the world on their *Glory Days* tour! Starting in Birkenhead and finishing in Japan in 2018.

2018

Little Mix toured the UK with their feel-good Summer Hits tour and released their fifth album, *LM5*.

2019

Woman Like Me won Best British Video at the Brits. The girls head out on their fifth tour, LM5.

2020

The band put their tour dates on hold as the world went into lockdown, but they still managed to release their sixth album later in the year, Confetti! Jesy decided to leave the band.

2021

Little Mix became the first girl group to win Best British Band at the Brits! They gave an emotional speech, thanking all the girl bands that had gone before them. Perrie and Leigh-Anne announce they are both going to have a baby!

2022

Confetti is taken on tour!

THE CONFETTI TOUR

The band have been itching to get out on tour ever since their shows were cancelled in 2020 and 2021. What can we expect from the *Confetti* Tour?

DISMAYED AND DELAYED

No one wanted The Confetti Tour to be delayed less than Perrie, Jade and Leigh-Anne. Originally due to start in April 2021, the band were forced to push back the tour for a whole year due to the Coronavirus Pandemic. The band released a statement telling fans how sad they were, but ended on a typically positive note: 'We can't wait to see you when it is safe to do so!'

HERE COME THE GIRLS!

THE CONFETTI TOUR WILL BE LANDING IN:

Belfast
Dublin
Newcastle
Liverpool
Sheffield
Birmingham
Glasgow
Leeds
Cardiff
Manchester
Nottingham
London

COSTUMES

As Little Mix's venues got bigger, so did their costumes! The ladies love to dress up and wanted their costumes to fill the room. Expect individuality, bold colours, glamour and most of all, outfits they can really move in!

JUST DANCE!

We know LM can sing, but their dance routines are just as fierce. We know the band will have been working hard to put on a perfect, banging performance for their fans. Each tour the ladies are joined by a troupe of amazing dancers, who help to fill the stage and put on the best shows ever.

SPECIAL GUESTS

Little Mix are all about helping other artists to shine. They have been supported by The Vamps and Conor Maynard, and this time round they'll be supported by winners of *Little Mix: The Search*'s Since September.

17

Bye bye JESY

In December 2020, Little Mix lost one of its original members when Jesy decided to leave the band. Whatever Jesy goes on to do, we know she'll do it in her own fierce style!

FULL NAME: Jesy Louise Nelson
DATE OF BIRTH: 14th June, 1991
STAR SIGN: Gemini

LITTLE MIX MAGIC MOMENT

Jesy has said one of the highlights of being in the band was performing at the Brits.

DID YOU KNOW

Jesy's documentary on internet trolling and mental health, *Jesy Nelson: Odd One Out*, won a National Television Award.

From Jesy

'I want to say thank you to everyone involved in our journey. To every single fan who came to see us in concert, who listened to our songs and sung their hearts out, sent me messages and supported me along the way. I love you all so much.' *

Did You Know?

When the girls saw Jesy for the first time at *The X Factor* auditions, they all thought she was really cool.

FROM PERRIE, LEIGH-ANNE AND JADE

'After an amazing nine years together, Jesy has made the decision to leave Little Mix. This is an incredibly sad time for all of us, but we are fully supportive of Jesy. We love her very much and agree that it is so important that she does what is right for her mental health and well-being.' **

*Instagram 14th December 2020   **Twitter 14th December 2020.

Who's your LM BFF?

START HERE

NIGHT IN OR NIGHT OUT?

NIGHT OUT

NIGHT IN

DISNEY OR MARVEL?

MARVEL

DISNEY

PAINTING OR BLOGGING?

BLOGGING

PAINTING

ROAST

PERRIE

If you ever had a problem, Perrie would be the first friend you'd message. She's fiercely loyal, just like you, and she'd be great at making you laugh, too!

Follow the flow to see who would be your perfect Mixer mate!

TAKEAWAY OR RESTAURANT?

TAKEAWAY

TRAINERS OR HEELS?

RESTAURANT

HEELS

TRAINERS

GOLD OR SILVER?

SILVER

BEYONCE OR RIHANNA?

GOLD

RIHANNA

BEYONCE

NACHOS OR ROAST DINNER?

VACATION OR STAYCATION?

NACHOS

VACATION

STAYCATION

LEIGH-ANNE

Grab your bag because you and Leigh-Anne are off to the shops. Your shared love of clothes and fashion would keep you busy for hours, while catching up on each other's news.

JADE

You and Jade would have the best sleepovers, filled with crafting, Disney movies and dance routines. She'd make you a lovely cup of tea in the morning, too!

Jade's Star Bakes

Not only is Jade part of the biggest girl band on the planet, but she's also pretty talented in the kitchen. Jade took part in *The Great Celebrity Bake Off for Stand Up to Cancer* and guess what? She won!

Round one

The first task was to create Fondant Fancies (those little cakes you get at parties). Jade made passionfruit-flavoured fancies, and although the icing didn't quite set, they still looked yummy! Judge Paul said Jade's flavours and textures were really good and her cakes were like rough diamonds.

> *I'll be starstruck when I see Paul and Pru, I'm a proper fan!*

THE GREAT CELEBRITY BAKE OFF FOR STAND UP TO CANCER

The Great Celebrity Bake Off for Stand Up To Cancer is a fundraising campaign created by Cancer Research UK and Channel 4. Taking part in SU2C Celebrity Bake Off was really important to Jade as, sadly, she lost her nana and auntie to cancer.

> *I am by no means the best baker in the world, but it's been such an amazing experience. It's been so much fun. If I can do it, people at home definitely can.*

Round two

Jade, along with her fellow contestants, had no clue what they would be baking in this round. After revealing their ingredients, they were given the recipe for a Cherry Lattice Pie and told to get going!

Jade hit a couple of bumps in this challenge, including not knowing what a lattice was and forgetting to make her custard (until presenter Matt Lucas reminded her!)

However, when judges Pru and Paul came to taste the contestant's pies, they put Jade in first place!

> This meringue has got me to breaking point. I never thought I would see the day.

Round three – The Showstopper!

For the show's finale, Jade had to make a 3D Biscuit and meringue scene that represented something she couldn't live without. Of course, she chose her bandmates and her fans!

Halfway through the challenge, Jade was finding her meringues weren't doing exactly what she wanted them to.

Luckily, fellow contestant Katherine Ryan was on hand to make Jade feel better and complete the task.

Paul said he was mightily impressed with Jade's creation, which included gingerbread mixers and a boiled-sweet set!

> I can't believe it. I'm in shock. My mam will be so proud. I might frame my apron, or start wearing it all the time to remind myself.

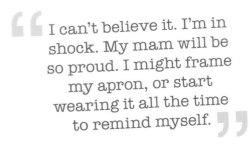

PERRIE LOVES THE LYRIC
IN WEIRD PEOPLE
"IT DON'T MATTER WHO
YOU ARE, YOU CAN BE
WHO YOU WANNA BE."

MIX KICKS

Little Mix need you to design them a killer new pair of trainers. Who will your pair be for?

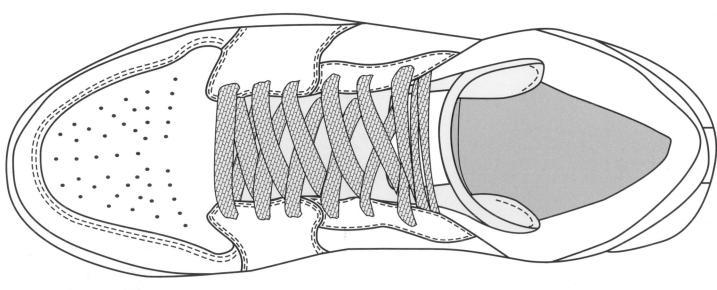

Little Lyric MIX UP

Something has gone wrong with these lyrics! Can you name the song, then put the lyrics back in the correct order?

SONG 1

So over this, so over you
Just 'cause I feel like
Thought you were gonna see me down
I ain't repeating you, so I'm deleting you from my phone now
I might go kiss somebody new
You ain't gonna see me cry

SONG NAME:

_____

LYRICS

_____

_____

_____

_____

_____

SONG 2

Come and get it
For Mr. Right
Need that magic
If you're lookin'
To change him over night
Here's the answer
While you've still got time

SONG NAME:

_____

LYRICS

_____

_____

_____

_____

_____

_____

SONG 3

And we're taking off
We don't need no camouflage
It's the female federal
It's who we are
If you with me, women,
let me hear you say

SONG NAME:

_____

LYRICS

_____
_____
_____
_____
_____

SONG 4

Sounded something like
I was just his tiny dancer,
he had control of my feet
He would lie, he would
cheat over syncopated beats
There was no song in the world
to sing along or make me move
Yes, when he came along,
that's when I lost the groove

SONG NAME:

_____

LYRICS

_____
_____
_____
_____
_____
_____
_____

LEIGH-ANNE:
RACE, POP & POWER

In May 2021 Leigh-Anne released a documentary about her experience of being a woman of colour in the pop industry.

HER INSPIRATION

Leigh-Anne always had a niggling doubt in the back of her mind about her place in the group. It wasn't until a trip to Brazil to perform that she started to question whether it was because she is mixed-race. In Brazil, the crowd went crazy for her, chanting her name over and over. When she looked out into the crowd, she realised it was mainly made up of non-white faces. She started to question her working environment, and in particular why she was often the only non-white face on video and photoshoots.

THE RIGHT TIMING

When the whirl of pop-star life came to a halt in 2020 due to the pandemic, Leigh-Anne finally had time to think about her concerns. She decided she wanted to use her platform as a member of one of the world's biggest girl bands, to make a documentary about her journey.

TIME TO TALK

Leigh-Anne's first stop was her parents, Deborah and John. They talked through their own experiences of racism and encouraged her to carry on with the documentary. Leigh-Anne then decided to gather together some of the most successful women of colour in the pop-industry, including Alexandra Burke and Keisha Buchanan. They agreed that there is still a problem in the media and music that needed to be addressed.

Keisha Buchanan

Alexandra Burke

BLACK LIVES MATTER

Over the summer, Leigh-Anne took part in the Black Lives Matter protests in London and got to talk to more young women about how they felt about racism in the UK and the lack of opportunities for people of colour.

SAIRAH
LEIGH-ANNE'S SISTER

PAVING THE WAY

Making the documentary was a brave and inspiring thing for Leigh-Anne to do. She learnt so much from the people around her and was inspired to start her own organisation, The Black Fund with her sister and fiancé, Andre Grey. The Black Fund aims to raise funds to help more people of colour to break into the creative industries.

COLLABORATION CELEBRATION

The girls have loved working with some of the biggest names in music – and they can't wait to team up with more superstars in the future.

MISSY ELLIOT
HOW YA DOING?

Release date: 15th April 2013

UK Chart position: 16

Did you know?
Missy Elliot first started making music in 1991 – the same year Leigh-Anne was born!

JASON DERULO
SECRET LOVE SONG

Release date: 3rd February 2016

Chart Position: 6

Did you know? Jason Derulo wanted to collaborate with LM after he heard them perform a cover of his song, *Want to Want Me*.

SEAN PAUL
HAIR 2015

Release date: 15th April 2016

UK Chart Position: 11

Did you know? The video for *Hair* is all about the band having a sleepover! It got nominated in the Best Video category at the Brits.

Perrie has said that her next dream colab would be with Chloe X Halle and Normani. Watch this space!

STORMZY
POWER

Release date: 26th May 2017

Chart position: 6

Did you know? Each of the Little Mixer's mums appear at the end of the video for *Power*!

MACHINE GUN KELLY
NO MORE SAD SONGS

Release date: 3rd March 2017

Chart position: 15

Did you know? *No More Sad Songs* is all about getting over a breakup and having fun again.

NICKI MINAJ
WOMAN LIKE ME

Release date: 12th October 2018

Chart position: 2

Did you know? *Woman Like Me* was co-written by music superstars Jess Glynne and Ed Sheeran!

SAWEETIE
CONFETTI

Release date: 30 April 2021

Chart position: 1

Did you know? *Confetti* is the first single the band have brought out since becoming a trio.

WIFI DROP OUT

You're streaming your favourite Little Mix videos when the WiFi goes. Nightmare! Can you recognise which videos are being played?

4

5

6

Fashion Now

Answers on pages 76-77.

Walk this way

Take a look at our favourite trio out for a stroll. Can you find the six differences between these two images?

How'd Ya Do?

 **LESS THAN 2 MINUTES** Smashed it!

 2 TO 4 MINUTES Meh!

 **MORE THAN 4 MINUTES** Epic fail!

Answers on pages 76-77.

35

Totally RANDOM

Did you know these totally random facts about LM? Fill in your own answers, too!

PERRIE

FAVOURITE PIZZA TOPPING:
Pepperoni and no cheese

FIRST THING THEY DO WHEN THEY WAKE UP:
Brush teeth

FIRST ALBUM:
Stacey Orrico

GREATEST STRENGTH:
Carrying on, no matter what!

FAVOURITE HOLIDAY DESTINATION:
Hawaii

LEIGH-ANNE

FAVOURITE PIZZA TOPPING:
Pepperoni

FIRST THING THEY DO WHEN THEY WAKE UP:
Check my phone

FIRST ALBUM:
Busted

GREATEST STRENGTH:
Being compassionate

FAVOURITE HOLIDAY DESTINATION:
Spain

YOU

FAVOURITE PIZZA TOPPING:

_____

_____

FIRST THING YOU DO WHEN YOU WAKE UP:

_____

_____

_____

FIRST ALBUM:

_____

_____

_____

YOUR GREATEST STRENGTH:

_____

_____

FAVOURITE HOLIDAY DESTINATION:

_____

_____

JADE

FAVOURITE PIZZA TOPPING:
BBQ Chicken

FIRST THING THEY DO WHEN THEY WAKE UP:
Have a wee!

FIRST ALBUM:
Craig David

GREATEST STRENGTH:
Keeping calm in stressful situations.

FAVOURITE HOLIDAY DESTINATION:
Florida

37

THE ULTIMATE
LM SLEEPOVER

If you've missed your friends over the past year, now's the time to plan some awesome get togethers!

THE INVITE

Photocopy this invite or copy onto paper. Add some bling with gems, sequins or glitter. Fill in all the deets, then hand out to your friends.

LITTLE MIX SLEEPOVER party

To:

You are invited to my sweet Little Mix Sleepover!

At:

When?

Party Checklist:

Sleeping bag / PJs / Toothbrush

SETTING UP

Decide with a grown up where you are going to have your sleepover. Whether it is in your bedroom or in a living room, make sure it is super-cosy. Put lots of cushions on the floor and create space for everyone to roll out their sleeping bags. Add some fairy lights and electric candles if you have them!

SNACK

A sleepover would not be complete without something to cure those midnight munchies! Fill a big bowl with popcorn for you and your friends to dig into and make sure you have a jug of water or fruit juice ready for your guests to fill their glasses and water bottles.

GAME GIRLS

Save the quizzes on pages 20, 46 and 74 to do with your friends. You could even come up with a Little Mix quiz to test your sleepover sisters on their Mixer knowledge!

CHOREO TIME

Pick a Little Mix track you all love, then look up one of LM's sick performance's online. Now, see if you can copy the choreo. Make sure there is plenty of space to dance before you begin and most importantly, have fun! You don't have to be perfect, as long as you are having a giggle - remember the band would have spent months perfecting those moves!

MICROPHONE
BLING

The band can't wait to get back to performing live! Colour in and decorate this microphone for their next show.

THE LYRICS
"NO MATTER WHAT YOU
SAY – IT WON'T HURT ME."
IN WINGS REALLY MEAN
A LOT TO LEIGH ANNE.

DM DILEMMAS

Can you work out who is sliding into who's DMs?

1

10:45 AM

< Back   New Message   Cancel

To:

What's up?

> I'm heading back up North to see my family for a few days, want anything?

Eye, get us a stottie! I miss them.

Send

Write message ...

BETWEEN JADE AND...

New Message 10:45 AM

Help! I need some fashion advice!

You've DM'd the right girl, what do you need?

New Message 10:45 AM

I've got to go to a fancy event and need a new outfit.

Hold tight, I'm on my way. Take a look at my clothing collection while you wait. I'll send you the link!

BETWEEN PERRIE AND...

3

New Message 10:45 AM

What are you up to?

Just about to watch a film, want to come over?

Sure! What are you going to watch?

New Message 10:45 AM

Aladdin, or the Little Mermaid, or Beauty & The Beast...

What about something non-Disney?

I don't understand that sentence.

BETWEEN LEIGH-ANNE AND...

Answers on pages 76-77.

LIFE IN LOCKDOWN

When their live shows, recording sessions and interviews got cancelled, Little Mix had to come up with something else to keep them busy!

PERRIE = TIKTOK STAR!

During lockdown, millions of people took to TikTok to cure their boredom. Perrie made some super-cute videos, racking up nearly 23 million views!

JADE = LEGO AND BAKING

Jade admitted that she was spending her time indoors playing with Lego and facetiming her mum to help with cooking. Let's hope she didn't get the two activities mixed up!

LEIGH-ANNE = PLAYING *THE SIMS* AND THE GYM

Leigh-Anne balanced out her time at home pretty well, by playing the computer game *The Sims*, and keeping fit by working out.

What's your CONFETTI TOUR ROLE?

QUESTION ONE

First up, time to decide where the band are going to play. How would you start planning?

A Find a map, print it out and pin it to a notice board. If you stare at it long enough, the places will just come to you. ☐

B Ask the band the places they really want to visit and go from there. ☐

C Make lists of where LM have played before, where they have never played, how many seats are in each venue, what the parking is like, what the food is like... ☐

QUESTION TWO

Jade gets stage fright just before the opening song. What do you do?

A Tell her to breathe, meditate or write her feelings down in her journal. If she doesn't have one, she can borrow yours. ☐

B Talk her through her fears, give her lots of reassuring hugs and hold her hand as she walks out on stage. ☐

C Give her a firm but fair talking to, and remind her of all the fans that are just buzzing to see her. ☐

QUESTION THREE

The designs for the new tour T-shirts have come in and they don't look good. What's the plan?

A Create something new. You can knock up a cool new design in no time. ☐

B Try and point out all the positive things about the T-shirt, rather than the negatives. ☐

C Put the T-shirts at the back of the merchandise stall and order more mugs, bags and pencil cases. ☐

QUESTION FOUR

Oh no! Perrie has forgotten the lyrics and her part is coming up soon! How do you help?

A Create a fancy lighting effect to distract the fans until Perrie is ready to sing again. ☐

B Start singing her part to jog her memory. ☐

C Tell the band to move on to the next song like nothing has happened. ☐

QUESTION FIVE

The tour is well underway, and the band are feeling tired. How do keep everyone's spirits up?

A Make everyone matching bracelets with the date and name of the tour on. ☐

B Organise a karaoke night. ☐

C Take everyone out for dinner. ☐

QUESTION SIX

How would you make the last night of the tour special?

A You would run around taking selfies with everyone, ready to make into a book later on. ☐

B You would tell everyone how great they were, and to make this night the best so far. ☐

C You would make sure everything was tidied up and everyone got home safely after the show. ☐

Mostly As

Your creative flair will really come in handy when you're thinking up some eye-catching costumes for Jade, Perrie and Leigh-Anne. You need to keep calm under pressure for those last-minute alterations, too!

Mostly Bs

You love performing, and you are super-supportive. You would fit right in with the cast and crew on tour, making sure that each show goes off with a bang and the fans have a night to remember.

Mostly Cs

Your organisational skills will be essential when it comes to putting together one of the biggest, brightest and most-exciting tours on the planet. From the running order to which venues the band will play at – you need to know it all!

Perfect pizza toppings

Make a delicious pizza for your next sleepover, grab some pals and recreate the Hair video!

ADULT GUIDANCE IS NEEDED FOR THIS ACTIVITY.

PERRIE'S PERFECT PIZZA

YOU WILL NEED

- ★ PEPPERONI
- ★ PASSATA
- ★ RED ONION
- ★ SWEETCORN

How to make it...

Spread the passata over your pizza base. Drain a tin of sweetcorn and carefully chop your red onion, then sprinkle on top. Now add your pepperoni and it's ready for the oven!

JADE'S BBQ CHICKEN

YOU WILL NEED

- ★ COOKED CHICKEN
- ★ PASSATA
- ★ BBQ SAUCE
- ★ MOZZARELLA

How to make it...

Cover your pizza base with passata. Chop or tear your chicken into bite-sized pieces and dot about. Now add a drizzle of BBQ sauce and finish with slices of mozzarella!

LEIGH-ANNE'S PEPPERONI PARTY

YOU WILL NEED

- ★ PASSATA
- ★ SPICY PEPPERONI
- ★ MILD PEPPERONI
- ★ MOZZARELLA

How to make it...

Start with your passata base and dot around your pepperoni. Finish off with slices of mozzarella.

What would your perfect pizza be topped with?

TOPPINGS

Little Mix
THE SEARCH

LM know just what it's like to go through a talent show in front of millions of people, so who better to front the search for the next big thing in pop?

THE SEARCH: Little Mix were on the lookout for a fresh new artist to support them on their upcoming tour. They searched through thousands of applicants and picked out their favourites to audition live. Here's what happened next!

THE BOYBAND

After picking their top 10 vocalists, Little Mix wanted to see how the boys worked as a group, and in front of an audience. Finally, they chose Talis, Lee, Zeekay, Adam and Kaci: New Priority

MIXED GROUP

The band were on the search for the next Steps or S Club Seven, knowing that a mixed pop-group could be big! Jordan, Rosie, Liam and Melina were picked and became Jasper Blue!

GIRL VOCAL GROUP

Little Mix knew exactly what each girl was going through, but they also knew exactly what to look for – that special chemistry that makes a girl band, great! They chose: Esther, Shanice, Tamara, Tyler and Mya-Louise: Nostalia!

VOCAL & INSTRUMENT BAND

The auditions cranked up a notch for this week as the hopefuls performed with guitars, keyboards and the swagger of a rock band. However, as well as their musical talents LM were watching to see how they performed together as a group. In the end, they picked; Matthew, Harry, Jacob and Patrick who became Since September.

GIRL DANCE GROUP

As the band trawled through audition tapes it was clear that some of the girls could really dance, as well as sing. So, they picked out the best to compete to be in the Girl Dance group. This was the most personal experience for LM as they felt they were choosing their own 'mini-me's! In the end it was Ellie, Aisli, Lauren, Megan and Liv who were picked to form Melladaze.

The final band to put together was the Rap R 'n' B group. With a mixture of soul singers and rappers, the auditions were an interesting and exciting process. After an emotional decision-making session, the final hopefuls who were chosen to perform on the live shows were; Romina, Versay, Eden and Ashley: YChange.

THE LIVE SHOWS

BATTLE OF THE BANDS

With the bands formed, it was time to take the shows live! First up, each band got to perform together for the first time, with each member of Little Mix giving them a score out of 25. When all the performances had taken place, it was mixed group Jasper Blue who fell short of making it into the semi-finals.

SEMI FINALS

Once again, each band performed for Little Mix, who gave their scores out of 25. Boyband New Priority and Instrument group Since September were left battling it out for the last spot in the final, with Since September grabbing victory with their final song.

GRAND FINAL

A spectacular final saw each band giving everything they had to two final performances. This time, Little Mix could only give advice as it was down to a public vote to decide who would be joining Little Mix on their next tour. In the end, it was the vocal and instrumental band, Since September who rocked their way into the nation's hearts.

CHRIS RAMSEY

Chris Ramsey had the job of presenting the live shows and LM thought he was the perfect choice. He reached the semi-finals of *Strictly Come Dancing*, so he was used to the pressure of live Saturday night TV. Not only that, but he comes from South Shields, just like Perrie and Jade!

Create
YOUR BAND

Do you wish you could be in a band just like Little Mix? Would you sing, play an instrument or dance? Use the space below to create your perfect band.

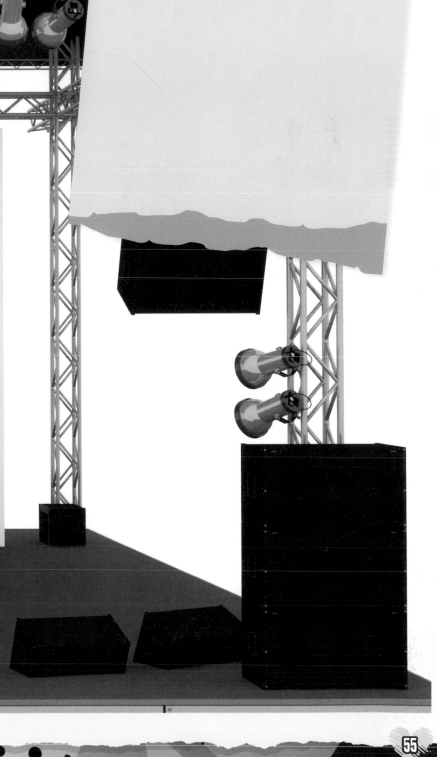

BAND NAME:

TWINNINGS

Find the perfect matches for these pictures of Perrie, Jade and Leigh-Anne.

Answers on pages 76-77.

57

Who's THAT MIXER?

Can you work out which LM lady is on stage in each of these pics?

1

2

3

PERRIE ☑
JADE ☐
LEIGH-ANNE ☐

PERRIE ☐
JADE ☑
LEIGH-ANNE ☐

PERRIE ☐
JADE ☐
LEIGH-ANNE ☑

4

PERRIE ☐
JADE ☐
LEIGH-ANNE ☑

5

PERRIE ☐
JADE ☑
LEIGH-ANNE ☐

6

PERRIE ☑
JADE ☐
LEIGH-ANNE ☐

7

PERRIE ☐
JADE ☑
LEIGH-ANNE ☐

8

PERRIE ☐
JADE ☑
LEIGH-ANNE ☐

9

PERRIE ☑
JADE ☐
LEIGH-ANNE ☐

Answers on pages 76-77.

MIXERS MAKING IT WORK

We all know Jade, Leigh-Anne and Perrie have conquered the music world, so what else have they sprinkled their magic onto?

ANYONE FOR A NANDOS?

In July 2020, Perrie became the face of South African restaurant, Nandos, and even shot an advert for its delivery service. As their most-famous sauce is called peri peri, our Perrie was the obvious choice!

KEEPING ACTIVE AND ACTING!

Leigh-Anne has produced her own swimwear range, been the face of sports brand, Umbro, and created her own fashion edit for online retailer, ASOS. Leigh-Anne has also filmed her first acting role, in British film *Boxing Day*.

FASHION AND FUN

As well as owning a bar and nightclub, Jade works with fashion-brand Skinnydip London. She has produced two collections to date including graphic tees, hoodies and super-cosy PJs sets.

ALBUM ARTWORK

Little Mix always come up with the best titles and sickest artwork for their albums. Now it's up to you to create album number seven!

ALBUM NAME

TRACKS

JADE LOVES THE LYRICS IN
IN *LITTLE ME.* SHE WISHES
SHE HAD SPOKEN UP AND
REMEMBERED SHE WAS
BEAUTIFUL WHEN SHE
WAS YOUNGER.

LM bullet journal

PERRIE IS A QUEEN BECAUSE...

you are A limited edition

JADE ROCKS BECAUSE...

LOVE WINS

LEIGH-ANNE IS EPIC BECAUSE...

WRITE IN YOUR THREE FAVOURITE LM SONGS

1.

2.

3.

IF I COULD ASK LM ONE QUESTION, IT WOULD BE:

THE POWER OF THREE

Three is the now the magic number for Little Mix!

TOUR THREADS

Guess what? The band need new outfits for their tour, and you get to design them!

The girls each have their own style, but they like to match too! Bring your outfits together using matching patterns or colours.

Make your colour palette here

Leigh-Anne likes crop tops, and they are great to dance in!

Jade goes for baggy elements and street wear.

Perrie often chooses trousers for her outfits.

The search IS ON

Find all the words from the list hidden in the grid. Words can go forwards, backwards, vertically and diagonally!

M	N	W	R	Q	C	E	N	N	A	H	G	I	E	L
E	V	P	O	S	I	T	I	V	I	T	Y	C	A	I
T	F	F	O	G	S	O	S	P	O	N	O	K	D	S
U	C	V	I	H	A	U	H	O	L	D	R	I	Y	P
L	P	E	R	R	I	E	C	W	G	O	E	A	E	I
A	G	Y	U	I	T	T	R	E	N	N	D	N	R	H
S	T	H	A	T	C	H	I	R	I	I	C	G	N	S
X	E	J	Y	P	I	J	I	E	L	A	A	H	E	D
H	Z	V	T	O	L	T	A	O	R	B	L	A	H	N
A	F	C	Y	L	T	O	H	P	E	D	A	J	D	E
I	M	K	R	E	A	S	M	T	T	E	P	A	A	I
R	N	L	F	E	M	E	E	E	R	R	N	B	O	R
R	P	N	R	S	E	P	N	N	O	I	H	S	A	F
F	O	I	E	M	A	H	I	M	B	C	O	B	R	E
C	I	B	L	A	C	K	M	A	G	I	C	E	Y	Y
G	Y	P	W	Y	D	O	L	E	M	T	E	E	W	S

- ☑ BLACK MAGIC
- ☑ CONFETTI
- ☑ FASHION
- ☑ FRIENDSHIP
- ☑ HAIR
- ☑ HATCHI
- ☑ HOLIDAY
- ☑ JADE
- ☑ LEIGH-ANNE
- ☑ PERRIE
- ☑ POSITIVITY
- ☑ POWER
- ☑ SALUTE
- ☑ SWEET MELODY

70

Answers on pages 76-77.

ALL THAT GLITTERS

Can you work out who these jewels belong to?

1

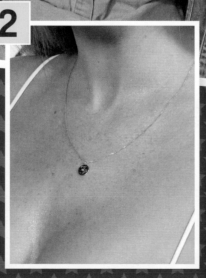

2

3

Leian

Peirry

Jade

Answers on pages 76-77.

YOU ARE EVERYTHING

Little Mix have been together, growing as a band for over 10 years. In that time, they've learnt how important it is to be your own best friend. Fill out this page of positivity and feel fabulous about yourself!

6 I'm all for whatever makes you happy, but never try to be something you're not. 9
- Perrie

6 I'm at the point where I am happy in myself, and I don't care what anyone else thinks. 9
- Jade

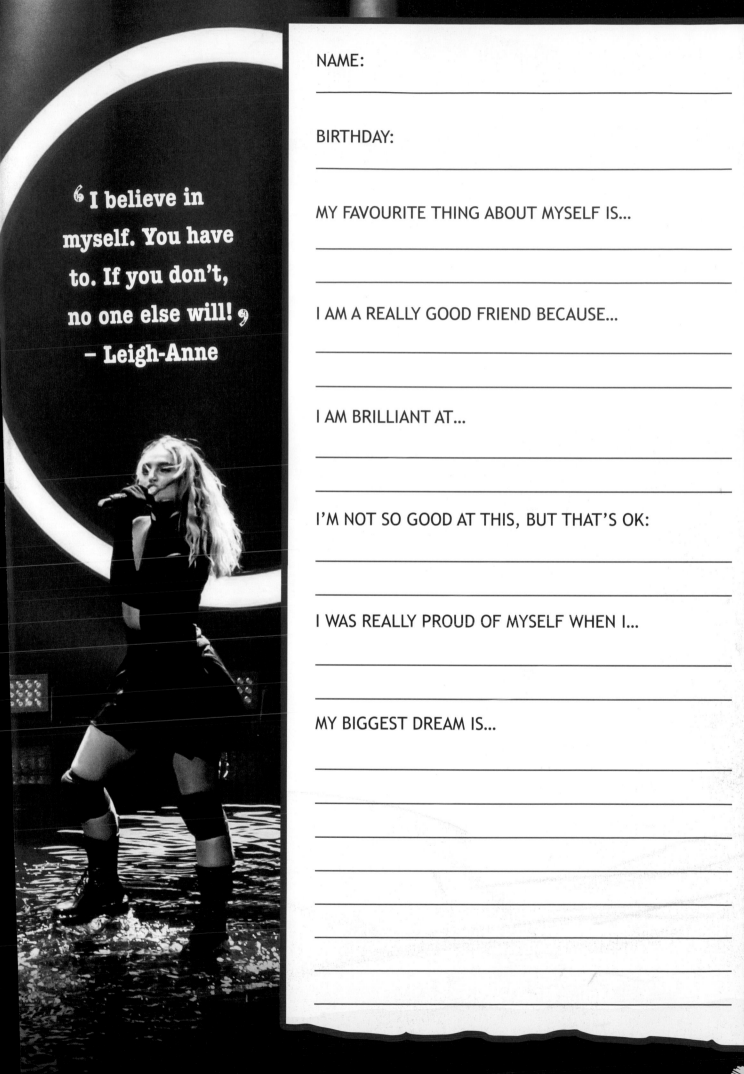

6 I believe in
myself. You have
to. If you don't,
no one else will! 9
– Leigh-Anne

NAME:

_____

BIRTHDAY:

_____

MY FAVOURITE THING ABOUT MYSELF IS...

_____

_____

I AM A REALLY GOOD FRIEND BECAUSE...

_____

_____

I AM BRILLIANT AT...

_____

_____

I'M NOT SO GOOD AT THIS, BUT THAT'S OK:

_____

_____

I WAS REALLY PROUD OF MYSELF WHEN I...

_____

_____

MY BIGGEST DREAM IS...

_____

_____

_____

_____

_____

_____

_____

The ultimate MIXER QUIZ

All the answers can be found somewhere in this book!

How much do you really know about the truly tremendous trio?

1 What does Perrie's mum call her freckles?

A Cuteness drops ☐

B Angel kisses ☐

C Beauty pops ☐

2 What is Jade's star sign?

A Capricorn ☐

B Aries ☐

C Gemini ☐

3 What is Leigh-Anne's pug called?

A Harvey ☐

B Charlie ☐

C Harold ☐

4 How many Brit awards have Little Mix won?

A 5 ☐

B 2 ☐

C 3 ☐

5 What type of pie did Jade make in *The Great Celebrity Bake Off for Stand Up to Cancer*?

A Apple ☐

B Cherry lattice ☐

C Lemon meringue ☐

6 Who did Leigh Anne interview for her BBC Three documentary?

A Beyonce ☐

B Rihanna ☐

C Alexandra Burke ☐

Answers on pages 76-77.

7 Who did Little Mix collaborate with on the *Confetti* single?

A Saweetie ☐

B Billie Eilish ☐

C Ed Sheeran ☐

10 What two things kept Leigh-Anne busy during lockdown?

A Baking and pottery ☐

B Learning French and cycling ☐

C Playing *The Sims* and working out in the gym ☐

8 Who presented *Little Mix: The Search*?

A Dermot O'Leary ☐

B Clara Amfo ☐

C Chris Ramsey ☐

9 Which restaurant is Perrie the face of?

A Nandos ☐

B Pizza Express ☐

C McDonalds ☐

ANSWERS

Pages 26-27

LITTLE LYRIC MIX UP

SONG 1: *No time for tears*

Thought you were gonna see me down
I ain't repeating you, so I'm deleting you
from my phone now
You ain't gonna see me cry
I might go kiss somebody new
Just 'cause I feel like
So over this, so over you

SONG 2: *Black Magic*

If you're lookin'
For Mr. Right
Need that magic
To change him over night
Here's the answer
Come and get it
While you've still got time

SONG 3: *Salute*

It's who we are
We don't need no camouflage
It's the female federal
And we're taking off
If you with me, women,
let me hear you say

SONG 4: *Sweet Melody*

He would lie, he would
cheat over syncopated beats
I was just his tiny dancer,
he had control of my feet
Yes, when he came along,
that's when I lost the groove
There was no song in the world
to sing along or make me move
Sounded something like

Pages 32-33

WIFI DROP OUT

1. *Holiday*
2. *Shout out to my Ex*
3. *Wasabi*
4. *Power*
5. *Love me like you*
6. *Break Up Song*

Pages 34-35

WALK THIS WAY

Pages 42-43

DM DILEMMAS

1. Jade and Perrie
2. Perrie and Leigh-Anne
3. Leigh-Anne and Jade

Pages 56-57

TWINNINGS

6

7

12

Pages 58-59
WHO'S THAT MIXER

1. Perrie, 2. Leigh-Anne,
3. Jade, 4. Leigh-Anne,
5. Jade, 6. Perrie,
7. Jade, 8. Jade, 9. Perrie

Page 70
THE SEARCH IS ON

M	N	W	R	Q	C	E	N	N	A	H	G	I	E	L
E	V	P	O	S	I	T	I	V	I	T	Y	C	A	I
T	F	F	O	G	S	O	S	P	O	N	O	K	D	S
U	C	V	I	H	A	U	H	O	L	D	R	I	Y	P
L	P	E	R	R	I	E	C	W	G	O	E	A	E	I
A	G	Y	U	I	T	T	R	E	N	N	D	N	R	H
S	T	H	A	T	C	H	I	R	I	C	G	N	N	S
X	E	J	Y	P	I	J	I	E	L	A	A	H	E	D
H	Z	V	T	O	L	T	A	O	R	B	L	A	H	N
A	F	C	Y	L	T	O	H	P	E	D	A	J	D	E
I	M	K	R	E	A	S	M	T	T	E	P	A	A	I
R	N	L	F	E	M	E	E	E	R	R	N	B	O	R
R	P	N	R	S	E	P	N	N	O	I	H	S	A	F
F	O	I	E	M	A	H	I	M	B	C	O	B	R	E
C	I	B	L	A	C	K	M	A	G	I	C	E	Y	Y
G	Y	P	W	Y	D	O	L	E	M	T	E	E	W	S

Page 71
ALL THAT GLITTERS

1. Leigh-Anne's necklace
2. Perrie's necklace
3. Jade's necklace

Page 74
THE ULTIMATE MIXER QUIZ

1. b   6. c
2. a   7. a
3. a   8. c
4. c   9. a
5. b   10. c

PICTURE CREDITS